6B Pencils

6B Pencils

Poetry

KAREN MOBLEY

RESOURCE *Publications* • Eugene, Oregon

6B PENCILS
Poetry

Copyright © 2024 Karen Mobley. All rights reserved. Except for brief quotations in critical publications or reviews, no part of this book may be reproduced in any manner without prior written permission from the publisher. Write: Permissions, Wipf and Stock Publishers, 199 W. 8th Ave., Suite 3, Eugene, OR 97401.

Resource Publications
An Imprint of Wipf and Stock Publishers
199 W. 8th Ave., Suite 3
Eugene, OR 97401

www.wipfandstock.com

PAPERBACK ISBN: 979-8-3852-2654-2
HARDCOVER ISBN: 979-8-3852-2655-9
EBOOK ISBN: 979-8-3852-2656-6
VERSION NUMBER 08/21/24

Climbing the Tower, *Lilac City Fairy Tales, Spokane, WA 2018*

I am Spokane, *I am a Town, project with Laura Read, former Spokane Poet Laureate, 2018*

In Celebration of Who He Once Was and Boarding Up the Closet, *Spokane Writes: A Poetry & Prose Anthology, Spokane County Library District, 2017*

You Might Never Eat Again, *Kitchen Fires, Spark Central, 2019*

Friendly Formidae, *The Thing with Feathers, Spark Central, 2018*

Spokane, WA129, Anthology created by Tod Marshall, Washington State Poet Laureate, Sage Hill Press, 2018

In memory of my parents, David and Marlene,
and my brother, Curt
Unwavering advocates for my art, writing, and spirit

Contents

In the deep pocket of my coat | 1
Pie in the Oven | 2
Humming | 3
Universal Gauge | 4
The smell—it was that smell. | 5
Does sadness? | 6
Allowing ourselves to burn: | 7
Catching Some Z's—My Night with Zorro | 8
The nerdy girls | 9
Lady Little Paw | 10
In Laniakea: A Cluster of Galaxies | 11
Six Minutes | 12
Friendly Formidae | 13
Shell-less Terrestrial Gastropod Mollusk | 14
In Celebration of Who He Once Was | 15
Counting crows | 16
33 Swans | 17
In the dark | 18
Circus | 19
The Refuge | 20
Dead Indian Pass | 21
Post-Surgical Musing: Sell me for Science | 22
Tidy Man | 23
Hot Tomato (Be Kind to Your Bartender) | 24
Colored Glass | 25

Moose | 26
I worship the scars from my injuries. | 27
Landslide | 28
Bear, bear | 29
Purple Cabbage | 30
Two cats share a sunbeam | 31
Iron Bed | 32
The Tiny Sadness (6B Pencils) | 33
Penitence | 34
You might never eat again | 35
April Fool's Day | 37
Boarding up the closet | 38
Some little snips in honor of Lenny Bernstein | 39
I did not know of odd and even numbers | 41
Spokane | 42
Ask me about the time | 43
Aunt | 45
Some observations on a hot August evening | 46
Forlorn Help—mission without probability of success | 47
Regeneration: By 2036 | 50
The sun is covered by the cloud. | 51
Into the center of the earth | 52
I am Spokane | 53
Climbing the Tower | 55
I invited everyone to the art show. | 56
I remember the flower : | 57
An Order to Save | 59

IN THE DEEP POCKET OF MY COAT

In the deep pocket of my coat, I hold a timid laugh.
I take your wonder, hold it in my hand,
small as a baby bird. I blow delicately,
raise the cover, show the red belly of wonder,
the tiny glee of pink pads on its foot.

PIE IN THE OVEN

You said, when I met you, a man's happiness lies in a woman's hand.
I thought of baking pie. I was searching for nourishment, milk for
 my mind,
apple pie for comfort. Happiness lies in the warm touch of fingers
affection shared by passing a hand forward and across a knee, me
 cutting
Jonathans and tart green apples, toward a back, moving closer
knee to knee, happiness is in the touch, lower, down the spine,
touching hair, skin. I am kneading crust, rolling, cutting a circle,
 carefully
sprinkling with cinnamon and sugar. A man's hand fits into a
 woman's body
perfectly. Your happiness lies in my hand, pie in the oven,
smooth skin against soft lips, holding your penis in my hand
touching the end to my palm, I push it into the cup of my palm
for a comfort, for a happiness that lasts for the duration of baking
 an apple pie.

HUMMING

A tree is humming. Along the path, walking closer
I discover it covered with bees. Bees sucking from
pollen of just broken flowers, like flying to a jar
of sugar, climbing into the kitchen to eat. Imagine,
the right of the jar, the circle that sets your eye,
the vortex that sets cowlicks in your hair,
the curl of my pubic hair,
a passion born the size of a bee swirls up
around the spike that holds my earth on its axis.

UNIVERSAL GAUGE

Do you love me down to my socks?

Yard stick, meter stick,
meter, clock, dial, rate, rank.

.2 inch
measure rain,
measure moisture,
measure tears,
grieving moves slowly
.2 of an inch
measure the sun
measure the ¼ of an inch of progress

leaves grow
wet roof
wet street
muddy road

electric meter
on the pole
numbers going
round and round

a stick pushed into tanks
to see how high the level is

rage
gauge
page

THE SMELL—IT WAS THAT SMELL.

The smell of the old empty house
with a leaky roof and a wren under the siding.

Grief sticks like a dependent animal,
too close, seldom faltering.

DOES SADNESS?

Does sadness hold its shape like a body, a glass, or a knife?
Bird on the horizon—one of flock or gaggle—without her kin.
A ravine, acacia, small green sprouts leaves.
I am waiting for the iguana to come out again.
That was the roughest road ever traveled.

ALLOWING OURSELVES TO BURN:

Some thoughts on burning the bush
on the Day of Pentecost

The sun is hot. It has been a dry spring.
The grass is thick and very dry. The fire danger is high.
We walk in the trees. My bush is wrapped around your
stalk, tall, hidden and stout. When you catch a strike
of lightning, catch on like a pillar of fire, speak to me
in tongue and tongue again. Let your flame flow through me.
Quicken me with your burnt offering. Kindle me with your
great sacrifice. Fuel me with your tree, your eternal heat.
And baby, baby, baby, burn my bush.

CATCHING SOME Z'S—MY NIGHT WITH ZORRO

I was looking for a horse. Quarter horse, graceful, thick, strong.
Like Trigger or Silver or Tornado. A horse that moves forward
like a galloping passionate lust. Moves inside like strong wind
or strong thrust, forcing his way like a righteous passion.
tornado like a fighting sword, pushing like a firm pointed trust.
But then I saw him. You see, it was the mystery,
The mask made me curious. Zorro, the fox, moving tall,
moving quietly like a coyote on the street. Zorro on horseback.
All I wanted was to capture tension the length
and strength of the horse's tail after a fly.
All that I wanted was to capture the volcano before eruption.
You see, it was the sheath, the taught hip, and the posture.
It was the sword. I was drawn to the sword.
A sword made for pushing, slicing, pulling in and out.
A sword for flexing my metal. For torching, hot, searing
delivering me from evil. You see, he had this dark hair,
dark eyes, framed by eyebrows and ears,
mask dark around his eyes. He just got me.
Zorro comes along and says, "Baby, whoa, you're hot!"
He says, "Baby, I'll take off my mask,
if you take off your blouse." I say, "No Dude.
I'd rather ride your horse."
I had been looking for a horse after all.
But on my way out, I trip on his sword.
I touched his sword. He cut me to pieces.

THE NERDY GIRLS

with glasses,
braces with headgear,
get together.
They would like to meet boys
learn to dance, even neck in cars,
they learn to use the compass
for navigation, sharpen knives with a whet stone,
ski, pitch a tent, provide emergency treatment
for broken legs, fix flat tires.
They have ideas.
They are like the boys.
They fish, ride bikes, tell jokes,
try to be ingenious.
They want to go to science fair.
They do not know
they have beautiful skin,
strength, limber muscles,
and senses of humor.
They think no one will love them
and they
will be
alone.

LADY LITTLE PAW

Holding Loosely

Holding loosely,
letting you be free,
holding loosely,
like the cat carrying
a live bird into the house
in his mouth like
my grandmother carries.
lettuce.

A small hand
little hand
grasping as if alive
grasping as if alone
grasping frail
arm sore from holding
on too tight
to stay alive
sore arm, no arm,
stroking,
no holding on
slipping into water
not being able to hold,
not attached,
not connected not too tight.

When I think of what I had
didn't have
what I held sacred
and tight and fully
Not knowing that I should have held
more loosely

It is hard to hold on in the rain.

IN LANIAKEA: A CLUSTER OF GALAXIES

With a nod to transfiguration (Matthew 17:1–8)

A complete change of form or appearance into a more beautiful or spiritual state

Fifty gallons of blood in your body. A hand that does not lie.
The Bible says it is dust to dust, maybe it is water to water.
Waiting is part of every story. Inside of every cell there is water.
The disciples wait for Christ. It is Lent, water rises up
and down the river, bodies, plump up, fill cells, our skins, our hearts,
baptism by spring runoff. The brain is 70 percent water.
Our lungs are 90 percent water. We gasp for breath.
We wait for babies to be born. Slap them to consciousness.
The dying wait for death's approach. The Lenten wait for resurrection.
The arrival of the Christ. The coyote waits to show off its howl to the moon.
I wait to grow a forgiving heart. In God's way, on God's way,

Laniakea, super cluster of galaxies, swirls dust, dust, dust.
The pinecone. It swirls into a vortex on its way to the ground.
Inside there is a seed, a fertile mother, a lovely cave with dark
murk. Listen, can you hear the waves on the shore of lake,
the small bird that cracks, whistles, and rattles, a dull hum
of a faraway ship, the laughter of the dead? Here, I watch for fire
to open the cone, for a tiny lady to run out with a bundle of wood,
sticks to stack and the squirrel to eat the seeds.
They can be eaten. Assurance of things not seen.

SIX MINUTES

I am orphan
infertile
standing alone

Six minutes is
not long

focus binoculars,
move cattle with horses,
saw, hammer, glue, and hoe

sharpen, shape
tape, tack

Six minutes is
not long to tell how

a birth defect,
a closed head injury,
broken fingers,
broken legs,
getting hit by a car,
shape me.

FRIENDLY FORMIDAE

In memory of Curt Mobley and Friendly Fred, the carpenter ant

So, the ants, they were your friends, right?
I knew many of them by their first names.
Fred for one. He was a friendly one.
He introduced me to his sisters.

Working together, ants never go
alone. Not ever. They looked kind.
Patient, prudent, temperate,
sterile, wingless with articulated waists
like 19th Century ladies.

Morasses, teeming hundreds,
social as one being,
trailing, a sticky line.
Flowing like molasses,
black, steaming.
with purposeful mastication
they chew up the house.

SHELL-LESS TERRESTRIAL GASTROPOD MOLLUSK

I hate how you remind me
of a clogged sinus. You move
quietly but I suspect that you
were coughed out of the lung
of a big mammal, a camel, elk
or a giant. I try to catch you
before you eat my garden, or
slime across the front walk.
I use your name in vain when
I speak of the lazy, the racist,
the misogynist, or the dog like.
Although they say this is an
insult to dogs. I don't like dogs
that much either because of poop.
Everything poops and you look
like poop. Dear Slug, I wish
I could love you like birds do
and enjoy the flavor the way they
enjoy earthworms, night crawlers,
and bugs. They pick you and your
kin off the driveway and swallow
with a gulp. I pick you up and
flush you like poop, with your soft
goopy skin and sucky, wet, dorsal
surface. Eww. I could say more
about your aversion to light,
your ability to shove yourself
into small spaces and your boldness
at night. You hussy.

IN CELEBRATION OF WHO HE ONCE WAS

He wears the ring on his right hand in
celebration of a marriage passed, two golden
retrievers, an old tabby cat, two kids
now grown, a vacation with a friend
who cooks on the old Coleman stove.
It was possible to celebrate
and be sad at the same time.
The way one can be perfectly happy
wearing the clothes of a dead friend.
This house once yellow; that house
once was white. A dog once named Murphy.
A cat named Sam. Another cat named Tiger.
A dog called Patch. There used to be a weeping willow
by the pond. That boy was a girl.
That girl wanted to be a horse.
This building used to be a factory, now it is a house.
I loved egg casserole and folding chairs.
I celebrate green trees, a hollow tune
mourning and low, slow, not quite a loon
the penny whistle played by a remembering man.

COUNTING CROWS

I count on the fingers of one hand, not enough to count
on the other, so I count to 6 and a half, a half, a half, and a half.

Right hand. Strong one. Able one.
Strong enough to turn the screw.

A bird was in my hand. I held it tight. It bled,
red head erases, my chest, the burning bush,
its feathers flame like Icarus. I let go. It flew away.

Looking at a dog with one ear raised,
the left listening ear, the right ear down
to keep the secret world inside,
a secret, still.

Crows soar.

33 SWANS

Hear
pygmy nuthatches
carpenter's hammer like wood
pecker, wood crackling in fire,
cackle of crow, the child's small
high
pitched
voice
swinging.

See
sun, shadows length
cars, buzzing at the end of roads,
plants, the earnest stretch of stalks,
lifting blossoms to the broken
stem
swinging wind
high.

Feel
fur, cats, hot sun on hides
awaken spring sun.
News carried
through wind,
shouted thunder.
her notes cursive, typed,
texted, spoken.

Salt
in our sweat,
ocean. Who knows me
and all thirty-three
swans
on their way
to Canada?

IN THE DARK

Down trees—the downed trees
frightened when they fall
how truthful in telling their story
round and round, the rings on their trunk,
the cracks and snaps
in the bark.

CIRCUS

In memory of Marlene

I'm going to join the circus
hop a train with elephants,
the short, the physically malformed,
the big cats. I will stand tall
in too short pants, lisp a little,
fling myself into air from a high wire,
jump at the chance.

THE REFUGE

At the house and in every truck, there were books. Peterson's Guide
to Western Birds, Roger Tory Peterson, John Muir, books with
    diagrams,
skeletons, beaks, diseases, corpuscles. Before I'd heard of Linnaeus,
    binomial
nomenclature, scientific method, or the Latin names for *Aves*.
Nothing flew or passed without being identified, counted, noticed.

Of course, others passed through—artists, politicians, dudes,
    hunters with
complex Italian names and fine guns. There was blood. Dead elk
    dripping
upside down. The hunter's blood—cut or shot—those came to the
    cabin so Mom
could pack their wounds with Kotex or gauze. Dad would drive the
    wounded to town
drop them at the hospital. As a kid, I knew names of muscles,
    veins, pressure points.

I knew God. He was called upon—loudly—to help with dying,
thanked for sun, moon, food, and the bourbon of a tired man who
    came back
from town with blood on his wool shirt and steel toed boots. God
    was thanked
for the woman, Mother, who was forever grateful for winch, tow
    chain, saw,
warbler and the calliope hummingbird with her tiny delicate feet.

DEAD INDIAN PASS

My cell phone doesn't work
out of range in the dead men's mountains.
Moose stand beside me, show their velvet.
Here is the rock, where I hit my head.
Here is the cattle guard, where my brother broke his arm.
Here is the hill, where Mom lost her binoculars.
Here is the place where Dad parked his truck.
Here is the tree, where the violet green swallows nest.
Here is the spring hill, where my parents' ashes
are scattered. And indeed, there will come a time
when no one
remembers.

POST-SURGICAL MUSING: SELL ME FOR SCIENCE

I stretch. I wait. I sit like an unlit candle.
Incisions—decisions—stitches—a few years from menopause,
Days from palm trees—tape—gauze—ice skates.
I am a little girl going to Beck Lake with mom to skate
in the flooded field where I skate in circles and circles.
Now an ice bag on my foot under an igloo.
At Rosauer's Supermarket, there are more African
Violets than there are in Tanzania. At my house,
there is a violet with leaves as soft as the cat's nose.
I throw it in the trash. It was beginning to mold.
The yellow house sits in stillness. Her people
are at work. The brown house stays silent. His
people are not speaking. Do you want my blood? I ask.
Why else would you put a tourniquet on my leg and drain it?
I already removed my hand. I sit in a post-surgical haze.
I have greasy hair, a sore body, and an unwashed face. I itch
under the gauze. I can't scratch. I feel nauseous.
In Switzerland, 4 million chocolate bunnies were burned.
$12 million dollars and a bunch of Easter bunnies are
out of luck, it says so in the paper. I get queasy thinking
about all those bunnies burning. Did you hear about the guy
in San Diego who selling people's arms $400 bucks per pair
- double for legs? Sold for science. I want to be cremated.
Don't sell me for science. I hate thinking of my messy being
laying around like a dead finch in my garden under
the rose bush. Do not cremate me until I am really dead.
And in Georgia, they find 300 people or more not cremated.
Why were those bodies just stacked like a cord of wood?
Murphy, the dog, was cremated, sat for years on Margaret's
coffee table in a plastic box and kept her company.
Who was this man Jesus? He was not cremated
but rose from the dead? What if somebody sold his body
for science? Oops, that was before science. Did you steal Jesus?
I think I see him. I think I see him now—
Jesus, ice skating in the candle's flame.

TIDY MAN

For H.

The tidy man lives in silence holding
his right leg. He sits in holey t-shirt and
little boxer briefs with blood on the seat.
He is coughing up the music of Germany
complete with oompahs. He spits death
out of his ears. There is a tiny rowboat with oars.
It is ready to row him into heaven. Unless he flies.
He thinks he might fly. He is dying
but there is no danger. None. None at all.

HOT TOMATO (BE KIND TO YOUR BARTENDER)

For Mark Miller

The bartender, is waiting for me
to step, to walk to the bar, grasp his hand, touch his thigh
and then ask him to go to the greenhouse where he raises
tomatoes. He knows how to stir the soil, heat up seed in a hot bed
to germinate in the steamy room. He wants me to grow tomatoes—
Early Girls, cherry, Roma, beefsteak—to give me ripe red fruit.
No, he's waiting for me to order a beer and with a beam
in his famous blue eyes turn my attention to gardening.
He says tomatoes grow best with a steady temperature
and we should avoid excessive heat, strong wind.
I ask him to go to the car, drive to the greenhouse
but we steam up the windows. He says, it's the stick shift
but I know, he wants me to eat those tomatoes straight from the
    vine.
No, Mark, the bartender, is waiting for me to shut up,
stop embarrassing him and tip him for a service well done.

COLORED GLASS

Colored glass, old shells, the wish bones
of chickens, glass eyes and blown eggs.
The woman has basketfuls of useless
objects from places where she has been,
dictionaries for languages she thought
to learn, but never did, bells to call people
who never came. She hangs the sun
on the wall which dims its rays.
She holds the waterfall
on top of her head.

MOOSE

I fell in love with the moose,
his velvet antlers and the gentle licking
of his tongue. He is tall. A nerd.
His high-water pants so charming
falling just below his knobby knees.
He is a big guy with a penchant
for wading slowly into a conversation
with a little food hanging from his lip.
I love that he tells stories of under water,
trout, and turtles. I adore that he loves Turnbull
and the Little Spokane. He can pick a goldfinch
out of the leaves on a fall aspen or call heron
in the rookery. He lays down to tell me secrets.

I WORSHIP THE SCARS FROM MY INJURIES.

See this here? This the place where I broke my leg
in 13 places, a baker's dozen of trauma. Here over
my eye, it's the wounded sight of hummingbirds,
a broken line of sight. My abdomen is covered
in small red scars as if something were to climb
from within. The biopsy scars are those of St. Sebastian.
I am sentimental about the breakups.
I cannot believe it has been over 30 years
since you abandoned me. It followed that I kept
choosing leavers. I am the girl with too many cats.
One to fill the hole of each loss. I live on the border
between the past and death, between nature and technology,
standing under a falling tree or a collapsing roof,
a moving fan or noisy heater, seeing inside like an autopsy.
The ghost of me wears a fur hat, sturdy boots,
flannel shirt. Hunt or hike. Paint on my shoes,
frayed and thin. Who were my ancestors? The people
of the spring, the hill with the burbling water.
The children say there are ghosts. They see through
the thin veil of clouds to the harsh glare of the future.

LANDSLIDE

It comes downhill so fast. No time to run.
I am flattened. I can breathe. I stand there,
my head sticking up. But then I couldn't.
That was all. I used to be someone. Now, mud
matters more. I stand with my head sticking
up waiting for the crows and the single buzzard.

I stood in the way of my work. I worry about the
sounds in the trees. The birds, the cracking branches,
the squirrel. My eyes move quickly to focus like a young cat.
The difference between lonely and lovely is only one letter.

BEAR, BEAR

For Carrie Wang's Laboratory Project—Postcards

Here on this bench where Connie went for her last outing
before she died, I dream I am a blue dragonfly.
Here at Manito Pond, I look for myself. I nap on
this bench, by the small Spokane bridge. I dream I am
small bird, finch, rail in the reeds, or a bear, a city bear.

In my dream, I call her name, entice her with bacon
food from a picnic. I cage my animal, my bear,
bear my grief, touch her fuzzy self. I come to this park
to watch the red winged blackbirds, three swans, six pelicans,
one osprey and heron standing with knees bent, listening carefully.
Come on. Walk slowly, will you?

PURPLE CABBAGE

In the midst of pandemic, devastating fires and my angst
about abandoning Afghanistan, I cheer myself with a purple salad.
Right on, you say. Its beets cooked, purple cabbage,
purple onion, purple beans, apple cider vinegar, basil.
It's the color of a bloody bruise.
It looks like it needs a bandage.

TWO CATS SHARE A SUNBEAM

I shelter in my place. I clean the house
in case I die, so it will be ready to sell.

I gave up eating cabbage so it would not
be afraid. We are afraid. For someone,
today is the end of the world.

Birds are migrating and so is the virus.
We celebrate the crown, the corona,
the glory of explosion, the sun
virus, perfect in its destruction.

I was hoping it was corvid
with a perfect murder of crows.

IRON BED

It started with the apricot tree,
followed by finding baptismal dresses
of those known to be sinners.

My grandmother went first.
She took a slow dive off her sewing machine
straight into the floor and injuring her brain
starting a cancer.

My brother flutters in the kitchen
like a moth against the window—never really leaving.

Mom and Dad always talked about good beds.
Bad backs, days of labor gave understanding
of mattress, a room that is not too hot or
hard on the ears. Roar of television forms
a comforting white noise. I used to sleep in silence.
Now I want stranger voice echoes in my lilting brain.

I hear wings flutter
over my grandmother's iron bed
where I sleep.

THE TINY SADNESS (6B PENCILS)

Today, I used up the last
of your 6B pencils.
All sharpened away.

At our aunt's house,
she put away
the pictures of you.

When I was small, I looked
up. I pointed my little
snub nose to you.

Shards of melted snow
men pierce the landscape
to the west.

Griffin fly flies no more.
Clouds fly free.
You, too.

That I believe.

PENITENCE

On the street of penitence and remorse, on a trip
to say hello or goodbye to the person I once was,
I walked and walked the street of patience.

I am sick, still, but I act as if I believe in God
floating in the land of in between sun and death.
I walked and walked the street of patience.

In the bottom of my shoe, there is a little mud
made with sweat and the dust of the streets I walk.
I walked and walked the street of patience.

It is lonely in my shoe, for no one is there except for
the rock that blisters my sole. My head is in the clouds.
I walked and walked the street of patience.

I drink coffee from tidy white China cups with saucers.
It is possible to be happy and lonely at the same time.

YOU MIGHT NEVER EAT AGAIN

Lentil soup. Dry lentil. Boiled. Garlic. Carrot. Salt. Eating alone, in the kitchen, nude under the air conditioner. No hock or bacon. No celery. No cracker. Oklahoma. In the Cruce Street apartment. Steamy. August. If I were another species, I might have chewed off my own hand.

Baking Powder Meatballs—One lb. ground beef, or elk, or deer, maybe antelope or bear. We'd never know what it was, frozen, stringy, and tough. Tough like my parents raised on ranches in Wyoming. They milked the cow to get the 2/3 of a cup of milk and a kick in the head. Two tablespoons of baking powder. Of course, use day-old bread, something stale. Add a whole onion. Everything mom made had an onion. I still eat an onion a day. Mom reminded us that onions kill germs, help to heal. As if we were sick, always. Two cans of mushroom soup for pretend gravy. Ball it up, cover it up, bake it in the oven at 350 degrees for 45 minutes. Pour yourself a bourbon. Turn on the news, say "How was your day?", smile politely, nod at the anchor man. Ask the person you're with if they still have chains on their car or have need of a crescent wrench. After the food is eaten, say kindly, "Did you get enough to eat?"

It always smelled like gravy. Grandmother always wore dresses and a checked apron with grease on her hips from wiping her hands. I still have her butcher knife, her old kettles, the maroon dinner plates with the hand painted flowers. She boiled the water on the stove. Look into the kitchen, see granddaughters standing on kitchen chairs washing dishes at the sink by the hand pump, chop the carrots one by one, by one. Stir the mushrooms, slowly and steadily. I can see the cups with saucers on the table after dinner with weak tea and tiny little sugar spoons. Like the tiny little fingers on my left hand, it has been a sad, tiring day, I want to chew things over with her once again.

Grandmother wrote this recipe complete with machination of substitution. If you don't have mushroom soup, substitute celery, or tomato, or cream of chicken. If you don't have onion, use garlic. If you don't have much to say, offer to help. If you can't help, turn to the other, put a little extra on the plate. You never know, you might never eat again.

APRIL FOOL'S DAY

You used to put on a fooling face,
the look you made when you were about to
pull a prank, tell a joke, tell a tall tale or a lie.
I wanted to pull a prank on you today but
you are still dead and there isn't anything
funny about that. Pranking the dead seems
a worthwhile effort for I'm sure the dead need
humor as much as the next guy.

BOARDING UP THE CLOSET

At her house, she was found boarding
up a perfectly good closet. If you
have a closet, you do not need a hole.
It wasn't the brain embolism that caused
her to start or the weird parasites under skin
in her arm by her watch band or the buried anger
along with the death pangs. Perhaps
it was the Holy Spirit or the red wine.
She stole six chairs and some pity
that was taken by her mother. She stuffed chairs
and pity into the wall and started
HAMMERING. She showed mercy on woodwork.
That cat, she didn't force it into the hole
despite its curiosity. It was like moving sand
one grain at a time. Slowly grieving
like chewing stringy meat. She planned to crawl
into the wall, like Jonah into the mouth of the whale.
She knew she could not board herself in.
She wanted to be a moth or a butterfly
holed up to grow wings.
Instead, she felt
too large
TOO LARGE
to have
an epiphany
or crawl
into
the hole
as ant.

SOME LITTLE SNIPS IN HONOR OF LENNY BERNSTEIN

With apologies to Verne Windham, KPBX

Dancer / Peer Gynt on the Radio (Edvard Grieg)

Skinny girl with a weighty man with sturdy arms slides back and up, tippy toes, tippy toes, sliding down and across, icy hill, waiting for swans, sea creatures, deep voiced crooning, skipping, slipping tippy toes, tippy toes, tippy toes. Touching his back with tiny fingers. Deeply swimming up and under the ice, whales, eels, and tippy noses on the bottom of the ice. Tall trees wave in the wind. Tippy toes slide across and forward. Across and back. Across.

Russian Sailor Dance (Reinhold Moritzewitsch Gliere)

Motors mufflers or whales? Swimming, pirouetting fellows and women, marching, twittering, oaring soaring, jingling, swimming, bam, bang, jingle, bam. rolling down a hill, really fast, sliding under a bush heart beats fast, breathe deep, bam. Bam.

Ritual Fire Dance (Manuel De Falla)

Metal, high pitched, yellow, red, blue, acid green
Underneath, two crashes, elk in rut, heads butt
Yellow bird, kinglet or warbler, twittering above
Climbing, walking, hovering bugs, elk crashing heads
Burnt umber darkness.

Oh!! so Nordic/ Peer Gynt (Edvard Grieg)

Deep walking in snow, ducks, geese
Step, step, step, into the blue cloud.
Deep, dark, yellow spots, flashes
Red and pop. Pop. Pop. Pop.
Clearing. Ducks. Slipping. Clapping.
Something is coming. It is big and mean.
It's going to grab us. Not now, but later
Sasquatch. Moose. Mysterious Mountain King.

Polka for a Golden Age (Dmitri Shostakovich)

Attitude, mice and cats, moving into little holes
Skipping into a forest, forest gong, banging, tweeting
Bump. Bump. Bump, Trumpets. Foreboding on
the edge, a large mammal, chasing, flirting,
yellow birds, slippy, slidey, bump bump bump
top and bottom and yellow, orange, blue, slippery
blue purple, elephant, mouse, dancing, circling,
Tweeting slow.

I DID NOT KNOW OF ODD AND EVEN NUMBERS

I did not know of odd and even numbers, how someone
could miss that those mountains are higher than seashores.
But then again, I once met a man in Central Australia
who did not know of oceans. I discover things that used to be
—timber houses, cedar shingles, tar paper, ringer washers,
and a leather collared dog. I am afraid. I do not have a gun.
I cringe and duck. Smoke clouds sky. We cough. Father grieves
the murder of his son. There is a panda toy strapped to a pole
by the highway. I saw it before my retina burned from looking
straight into the sun. Fires burn around us. Scientious people
pretend. One in four believe the sun rotates around the earth.
Some want to understand dinosaurs—triceratops. It is false
that the rain follows the plow. Squashed thumbs are probable.
Scavenging swine pass through the city, eat up what is not thrown
into the river. My gallstone is an inner noon pulling toward
my chest. There is a robin in the space between the door
and screen door. People chase the sun and her eclipse. The sun
goes around and around or so we think. The mouse is in a metal
bucket, running in circles, trying to get out.

SPOKANE

Do not eat more than two fish a week from the river of murk. Bill, the Fauceteer, master of old plumbing parts crowns with copper pipe. Tormino's Glass man makes seductive proposals while windows are measured. White's Boots steel the boots toes. Miller's is unsurpassed in hardware. Someone here knows how to sing the Battle Hymn of the Republic. Our state is named for George Washington, President of the United States. I don't know if his teeth were really made of wood. May Hutton was a suffragette. Mrs. Browne started theatre and all that shameful dancing. Lewis and Clark came by. Thompson explored. Cowley started the first church. In 1893, there was a wheat panic. The Great Spokane fire burned the town. Mr. Duncan brought lilacs. In Manito Park there used to be a lion in a cage. At Drumheller Spring, Spokane Garry taught. There is a meteor hole filled with trash and norovirus at the homeless shelter. A man digs up ant hills looking for gold. In Washington, the loss of grasping is worth more than in Oklahoma. $118,266. It says so on this chart. The French horn player says naked ladies are okay. Someone remembers what it means to be a tree. There are more than a few dogs named Jake. There is a place called Z Nation near here. The Monroe and Washington Street Bridges fell into the river. The Governor was mauled by a bear. There are soldiers buried west of town near a place for those who wander downhill. Water is held in the cleft of the rock. In the old days, things were thrown into the river to wash downstream—sawdust, garbage, chamber pots and offal. The Japanese Garden was built in 1961. Our children ride around town on metal goats and carousel horses going round. If you dig down, you might find the bones of salmon or Chinese in opium dens. If you turn carefully, you see the cursed ghost of Jimmy Marks or the naked ass of Willie Wiley. Drink in the meth and the bootlegged whiskey. No, not all Indians make totem poles. Heron stands still through it all. Amen.

ASK ME ABOUT THE TIME

After Manaya Winter

Ask me about the time my brother tried
to jump the cattleguard with his horse
or when my father picked me up, arms
outstretched, or my mother chased us
around the house laughing. Their shadows
chased me through the trees, across
the prairie, along the creek, to my house
filled with their possessions. I offer myself
as small pieces of them, attempt to create
family where none remains.

Ask me about the time my brother disappeared
moved to California and began again without
us. My dad confused about why he tried
to become a cartoonist, jumping the traditions
and meeting girls through the classifieds and
living a city life. We stayed apart until Curt was
sick and died in ICU without explanation.
His shadow followed my mother to her end.
My father foundered soon after leaving me
to create family where none remains.

Bit by bit. The world took chunks of me as they
left the world. Ask me about the first time
I had Christmas without family, or the
many attempts to drown my grief in turkey
and gravy, stuffing, and wine. The way I couldn't
stop talking, how it seemed impossible to fill
the void. I drowned in the pain and didn't return
until you left me to live here in this house alone.
Bitterness buried me, grief flooded, marooned,
I was forced to become someone new without
a family. None remains. The shadows hold.

Ask me if I've ever had to use pocketknives
and screwdrivers to make holes in my heart to let
out the anguish. There isn't a tool left
to use. They cannot find their way. Back.

Home. Ask me if I can still hear their voices.
There is nothing more holy than becoming a ghost.
I call you but you are dead

AUNT

Andrew has learned to play catch
with the red mouse. Marie eats flies.
Betye sits in the morning sun. The small
green leaves emerge out of the branches.
It smells of mourning
coffee, car exhaust, rain, bacon.
I live in the growling shadows.
I don't have a picture of you smiling.

SOME OBSERVATIONS ON A HOT AUGUST EVENING

The smoke is getting to me. I saw the crows come down out of the sky.

They soared over the stage, scattered when the clarinet player began to play.

It was smokey. The drummer was bald. I was not alone. I belong here,

along the westward highway, with its taco trucks and patios. I drive aimlessly

looking for work, rivers, sweet deer with their antlers in velvet, birds

diving into rivers—osprey and eagle.

This is a fabulous year for sunflowers. It's a sad year for trees. Heat stress and aging.

Death but good food for woodpecker and ants. The sweet guy at LaPresa in Coulee Dam

told me to come tomorrow for flan. If you are in Coulee Dam tomorrow stop by and tell him

Karen is waiting for flan. I was disappointed that they were out. Remember to drink water.

It's going to be hot tomorrow. Be present with the sun, she makes the shadows.

It is forbidden to gawk at the elephants.

FORLORN HELP—MISSION WITHOUT PROBABILITY OF SUCCESS

Why are there no quarters in the drawer?
Why has no one shoveled the sidewalk?
The snow gentles everything. I want fluff and sparkle.
Silence. A few twittering birds. A pinecone falls to the roof.
We are counting the days of our lives. Three days until Christmas.
Ten days to the end of the year.

*

Born that way
It could be cancer, but it could
be that I was born that way.
Everything on my left side is messed up.
My leg, my arm, my heart, my eye. The left
side is weaker. I try to run away from myself.

I stay home and try to be in love
with the cats and the house plants.

My left side is colder than my right side.

*

I had a mammogram on Monday.
They called today to schedule another.
A radiologist will talk to me.

*

I read the diagnosis. Asymmetry. Density.
Invasive Ductal Carcinoma.

*

On the day, I learned of my cancer
I read the Pacific folding door spider, *Androdiaetus*,
hides in the folds. My cancer is hiding under
bend, and thickness. Perhaps cancer of the folding
door.

*

The Nebra sky disc will be exhibited at the British
Museum. The disc is bigger and heavier than my cancer.
I envision the disc as my shield, covering my breasts with
blue-green bronze and gold. My sun or moon, my lunar
crescent, and stars. Marking the solstice, marking my transition.

*

A man buys a triceratops for "personal use."
Perhaps if I had a live triceratops, it could
eat the cancer whole.

*

Grandmother stayed in Salt Lake City
while she had cancer treatment.
Young mother and children in poverty
with worries; husband on the ranch
bills to pay, cattle to feed, haying.

*

It's okay, until it isn't.

*

Kill the phantom limb of a forlorn hope.
Oh come. Oh, Come.
Migrate to me with the monarch.
Stand with me talking to strangers.

*

I'm ill and I'm trying to maintain a connection
to what little family I have. I am not trying to do
anything to you or your people.

*

Does everyone hurt? Are all the backs and eyes tired?

REGENERATION: BY 2036

I will live alone until I die or move to assisted living.
My stomach is always upset. My heart is always broken.
The doctor asked if I sleep sitting up. I've slept sitting up for years.
I'll retire anytime now. I will throw away the clothes of the dead.
The heart beats 100,000 times a day, 700,000 times in a week,
roughly 35 million times a year. My heart beats for the dead.
I will make a new friend. Virtually all astrobiologists believe
we are not alone. We will make contact with intelligent life
by 2036. We will meet other life forms. We will recognize them
when they grow before our eyes. It smells of rain
on the hot floor of the pine forest. It's cloudy all the time.
I'm using binoculars. Swallows circle overhead.
My mom would roll up the legs of her jeans to fish
in her Ked's. She would roll up her pants to get sun on her feet.
She'd watch for sandpipers, ouzels, and killdeer.
Snipe. I see them for her. If I could grow a new hand, would I?

THE SUN IS COVERED BY THE CLOUD.

It's obscured by mist. What we have lost,
we never really held. Our grasp is frail.
We cannot hold. What is lost,
may be found, left for dead.

INTO THE CENTER OF THE EARTH

He told the family what had happened.
My hands, the grip, failed me.
I fell into the center of earth
without even a ribbon to break my fall.

I AM SPOKANE

I am Jingle Boy, the cat with tag and bell
I am the Ridpath with jazz singers on the roof top
I am the bridges falling down
I am the mills on the river, the farmers in the field

I am the heron at Manito Pond, the moose along the Latah
I am the lilac princesses of 1998
I am the hill to the hospital overseeing town
I am the swinging bridge to the island where they dumped the chamber pots

I am breakfast at the Satellite
I am Dicky playing piano, Mark playing a glass with a dirty yellow spoon
I am the old Monkey Wards where the city council meets
I am the booze joint and the drag club, Miss Mylar on the mic

I am the Klemmer, the State, the Met, the Bing
I am the Fox, I am burlesque queens and boxers
I am the skaters under the freeway
I am the salmon caught in baskets

I am the street where suffragettes marched, where we protested Vietnam
I am the naked beach at the People's Park
I am lilacs and roses in the garden
I am Willy Wiley petting a raccoon

I am the marmot eating Cheetos off the chest of the naked man
I am the ponderosa pine dropping needles on the ground
I am the wind blowing farm dust, west to gust
I am drunks standing by the freeway, pilots at the airbase

I am the women with grenade launchers in fussy lilac dresses
I am a margarita at the Baby Bar, a poem in the mouth
I am the giant stacks at the Steamplant by the railroad and its track
I am the children feeding the garbage eating goat

I am Dixie on her bicycle and George burying drawings in the park
I am chickens at E. Sprague Northwest Seed and Pet
I am ravioli at Cassano, Pho at Vien Dong
I am beer and Irish Whiskey

I am Spokane

CLIMBING THE TOWER

For Harold Balazs

It is possible to be happy and terrified all at once.
That was how I felt as I started to climb, shaking,
gasping for breath as I got higher and higher into
the air as my hands sanded raw on concrete.
I knew if I got to the top after climbing up the zigs
and the even higher zags, I was going to see the
creed. As I was climbing, I thought about all the
towers, the Steamplant and her giant towers of
smoky sex, the big clock tower across the park.
I am always climbing to the tallest place like
a cat who wants to be in a tall tree, on the roof
or top of the refrigerator. I want my own turret
on top of the Ridpath right under the P where I can
look down into the downtown like a pigeon.
I walk around the base of all tall things before I climb
in a little ritual, counterclockwise, smiling like Cheshire cat
hoping, worrying that I might have to go down into a
dank, dark basement, into the land of leaking sidewalks,
mold, singing small frogs or into the beigeness
of a bureaucracy. What belongs in this poem is a monster.
We have one in the White House. This tower could have a
Rapunzel but right here at the top it has a creed,
Transcend the bullshit.

I INVITED EVERYONE TO THE ART SHOW.

The art was on the floor, paint
slipped off the canvas, piled right
next to the baseboards in slimy piles
of red, green and blue, like cow pies
right against the wall. The smell was
overbearing, the solvent, the sweaty
bodies, the riff of farts or warm cheese
on the table next to the crackers, white
wine and the sweet little square napkins.
There was a cat under the tablecloth
waiting for us to drop food, grab and run.
We were standing, waiting for the president
And his wife who was wearing a coat
the exact color of the cat's fur. It was
finally clear. The smell was fear—our fear,
the cat's fear, the paintings' fear of failure.
The heart's fear of being too cool, the sun's
fear of being too dim, the concrete's fear
of breaking under the weight of the big
truck with the men with machine guns,
the limos arriving. The fear of the president not
knowing what to say about this art in drooling
piles all around the walls like cow pies and the fear
of the president's wife who neither liked the
president nor her cat hair coat.

I REMEMBER THE FLOWER :

With a nod to Laura A. who sent the email inspiring this poem

Seeds need to be grown. Seeds age. Thousand-year-old seeds can germinate. I keep my seeds cool. White Hutterite soup bush beans. Grandma Walter's pole bean. Paint or Yellow-Eye. Inchelium Red is garlic. Nootka Rose is from the San Juans if I remember. You all have heard of Walla Walla Sweets and Cannellini white runner beans. Italian. Iranian veggies and fruits. Dragon carrots. You can't eat carrots if you want to save seed. Poke cherry tomato. Sweetie. Small. Brad's atomic grape tomatoes. Jalapeno. Bell peppers, red or yellow. Cantaloupe, Hearts of Gold, Spokane Valley. The Spokane Valley used to be the apple capital of Washington State, too. Now they just grow houses. Minnesota Midget is for northern climates. Delice de Table is a French melon. Melons will not cross-pollinate with watermelons. Sugar baby. Blacktail Mountain. Developed in Idaho. 70 days. Watermelon is native to Africa but was brought to the American Southwest in the 1500s. Iranian watermelon is called Ali Baba. Our growing season is too short. Early Moonbeam are good for northern climates. I adore pumpkins. They are beautiful, edible, diverse, decorative, and last. You can make so much food with a pumpkin or squash, really, breads, soups, pies, lasagna, custards, cheesecake. Eat them roasted. Eat their seeds. Here are good things about open-pollinated squash. They are not hybrids so you can save the seed and the seed, when planted, is true to the form of the parent. You know what you are getting year after year. Planting the same variety over and over acclimates seeds and plants to growing conditions. You don't have to buy seeds every year. They can cross pollinate. You can get some funky squash. It may taste good, but it may not. Squash should be planted a quarter mile, maybe more from other squash. It can be a challenge in the city. Squash is in the genus Curcurbita. There are four species categories: Moschata. Pepo. Maxima. Mixta. Most of mine are in the Maxima. Zucchinis or Cocozelles are in Pepo. Zucs are prolific. If you grow them, pick them early and often. It's amazing how big they can get quickly. There is an old joke about making sure to lock your car doors at religious services or else you will find zucchinis in your back seat. Cinderella Pumpkins. I have seeds for Jarrahdale pumpkin. It's green, beautiful, from Australia and good tasting. And I have Lakota Winter squash that is orange and green. Acorn or spaghetti squash. Brussels Sprouts. Leeks. January King Cabbage. Detroit dark red medium top beets. Five color silver beets. White Lisbon bunching onions. Red Deer Tongue lettuce. Quatre Saison lettuce. Rustic Arugula. Spinach. Butter crunch lettuce. Chives. Dill. Eiffel Tower lettuce. Bloomsdale spinach. Blue borage. Tom Thumb lettuce. Marvel of 4 Seasons butterhead lettuce. I can deliver seeds in person or on doorsteps. You can't eat greens if you want them to go to seed. That is the value of planting several plants of the same variety. Some could cross pollinate but I have not seen it happen. You can plant in successive waves. I need to divide French tarragon, chives, mints, and others I can't think of off the top of my head. Plus, flowers, and Yellow Rose of Texas cuttings. I don't have cucumber seeds for eating or pickling. I don't grow eggplants, but I love them. The rest of the family is not keen on them. The best eggplant I have eaten was in Sicily. We have many flowers. Small purple irises. Amaryllis. Bells of Ireland. 4 o'clocks. Hollyhocks. Hyacinth Bean. California poppies. Morning glories. Columbines. Cosmos. Coneflower. Zinnias. Queen Anne's Lace. Kiss-me-over-the-garden gate. Sweet Williams. Black-eyed Susan. Cornfield poppy. Violas. Purple bearded irises. Bishop's weed. Lily of the Valley. Grape hyacinths. Ask me. I have not checked in with Jerusha about what she is planting this year with all her seeds. I remember flowers.

AN ORDER TO SAVE

Save something for a rainy day.
Save for the rain. Today
would be a good day to save for.
The sun rises in the east.
It is light enough to share
with egrets, eagles, and
ascetics. It is singing rain.
I saved my mother's love
stowed it in the deep pocket
of my coat like a river rock
put it close to my heart like
a red breast of robin. I put
my mother's love in the car
with the sled and grandmother's
dishes. I put aside the head of
purple finch grieving.
An order—do not resuscitate.
Grief is not contagious.
But save it. Save it until it rains.

www.ingramcontent.com/pod-product-compliance
Lightning Source LLC
Chambersburg PA
CBHW061247040426
42444CB00010B/2281